Andrea Almada
Illustrated by Becky Radtke

A Harcourt Achieve Imprint

www.Rigby.com
1-800-531-5015

Literacy by Design Leveled Readers: *Under Lock and Key*

ISBN-13: 978-1-4189-3791-1
ISBN-10: 1-4189-3791-6

Printed in China
4 5 6 7 8 0940 14 13 12 11 10 09

Tuesday, January 28

Dear Diary,

Today I couldn't wait to rush home from school and write all of my most secret and exciting thoughts here for the first time. Whenever I flip through your blank pages, I think about all the things I will share with you. I'm so glad you have tons of pages to be filled because now that I'm older, I have so much to say. I got a new set of fancy pens that I'm going to use to write all of my most secret thoughts!

Dora

Wednesday, January 29

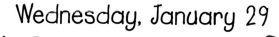

Dear Diary,

Since you and I are going to be best friends, I think you should know about my family. Mom and Dad are cool, and my grandparents, who live in the house behind ours, make the best *churros* and hot chocolate in the world. Then there are my two nosy brothers, Omar and Carlos, whom I hope you'll never meet. They love to snoop around in my room and always get in trouble for it. I hid my last diary in the bottom drawer of my dresser, but they still managed to find it—twice!

After the second time, Mom made both of them write me letters saying they were sorry, so hopefully they've learned their lesson. I'm going to hide you under my mattress this time. And I'm making sure that you have a good lock and key, just in case they decide to snoop again. I'll hide the key somewhere special, so there is no way they'll ever get to read you. It's just you and me—and our secrets.

Dora

Dad   Mom   Carlos   Omar

Grandpa   Grandma   Chico

Thursday, January 30

Dear Diary,

Now that you know so much about my family, let me tell you about school. My best friend Daisy and I have been in the same class since kindergarten, but we knew each other even before that because our mothers are friends. My good friend Nath had always been in my class, too, until this year—so now I only see him at lunchtime. I'm in the fourth grade now, and I really like my teacher, Mr. Fong, because he makes school fun with his silly jokes about his days in school.

Me Daisy Nath

Today I got all the answers right on my math quiz. Math is my favorite subject, but I like gym, too, especially when we play soccer. Last Friday in gym class we had a soccer game, and I scored three goals! I was so tired after all of that running around that I could barely walk. My friends offered to carry me back inside, but they were just kidding!

Dora

Sunday, February 2

Dear Diary,

Daisy's parents went to Atlanta, Georgia, this weekend for a wedding, so she stayed at our house for two nights. I love it when she spends the night because we get to stay up late, giggling for hours together. We always do something special, and this time Mom let us paint our nails with pink glitter nail polish. Then Mom, Daisy, and I baked a big, strawberry-flavored cake, and we let Omar decorate the icing with candy.

Omar wouldn't stop adding candy to the cake, and the candy was so heavy that it almost crushed the whole cake! Dad said that it looked magnificent but tasted a little too sweet in his opinion. Omar thought it was perfect, and Daisy and I just laughed. We had such a good time, and I would be so happy if she were my sister. I've always wanted a sister to give me a break from my two younger brothers.

Dora

Monday, February 3

Dear Diary,

Daisy called me early this morning to say that she wouldn't be going to school because she had a bad cold. I usually eat with Daisy, so at lunchtime I looked around the cafeteria for someone else to sit with. I was going to sit with Nath, but then Lucila, the quietest girl in class, asked me to sit with her. It's strange that we've been in the same class for three years, yet we've never eaten lunch together.

"I'm very shy, and sometimes I'm not sure what to say when I'm with a group of people," Lucila confessed to me when we were eating together. But I could tell that she has a lot to say and that she's really interesting. We have a lot in common because she loves soccer, too, and she just joined a soccer team. I told her that she should definitely sit with Daisy and me tomorrow at lunch.

Dora

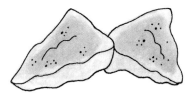

Thursday, February 6

Dear Diary,

Lucila has been hanging out with Daisy and me at lunch every day this week, and she really livens things up. Today we treated each other by bringing special snacks to share, and we sat outside under the shade of a tree for lunch. I thought carefully about what to bring and finally decided on crispy tortilla chips and Grandma's spicy salsa. Lucila shared her favorite food: sopapillas covered in cinnamon sugar and sticky honey. Daisy filled a big thermos with her Mom's ice-cold lemonade and shared crunchy celery sticks smeared with gooey peanut butter.

We stuffed ourselves by eating every last bit, laughed until the bell rang, and almost gave ourselves stomachaches. Lucila doesn't seem so shy anymore. She's just like us—silly and fun. I think that soon I may even have *two* best friends!

Dora

Saturday, February 8

Dear Diary,

I was so excited today when Daisy and Lucila met me at the school's soccer field. I knew that a Saturday morning playing soccer with them would be much more fun than playing with my two brothers. Carlos always wants to outrun me, and Omar tries hard, but he can't seem to kick the ball straight. Playing with them is exhausting because they are all over the field.

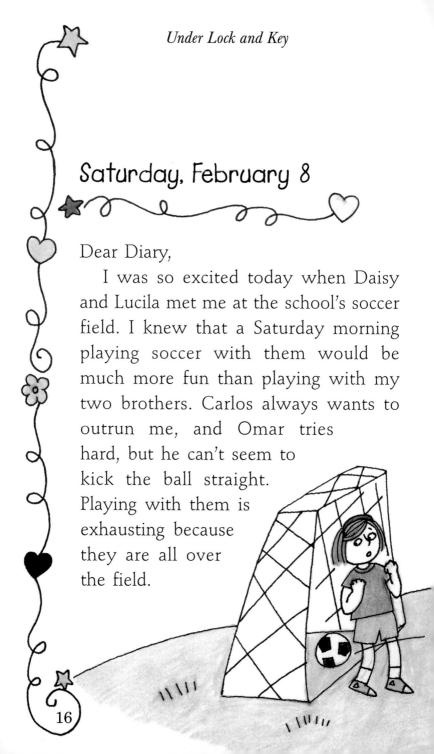

Daisy agreed to be the goalkeeper so Lucila and I could play against each other and try out our new moves. It wasn't long before I found out that Lucila was a much better soccer player than I. I thought Carlos was fast, but I had never run so hard or so fast in my entire life! The worst part is that after trying so hard, I didn't even win—Lucila scored two more goals than I did. I wonder how that could have happened.

Dora

Sunday, February 9

Dear Diary,

I can't stop thinking about the soccer game on Saturday. I think Daisy might have tried harder to block my goals than Lucila's, but why would she do that to me? Daisy would never help Lucila win just so I would lose. I should stop worrying about this and be happy that I learned some great new moves by watching Lucila play.

Maybe Lucila is just really good at soccer and has learned a lot of new tricks playing on her team. She did seem to run a little faster than I did. We both attempted to score many goals, but Lucila managed to get the ball past Daisy more often. I wonder if Daisy was not blocking Lucila's goals as often because she likes her more than me now. But how could she do that, when I'm supposed to be her best friend?

Dora

Monday, February 10

Dear Diary,

You won't believe what happened yesterday! I left you out on my bed after writing to you, and my sneaky brothers came in and got you! I had locked you up, luckily, so all they could do was tease me and wonder what was inside. I complained to Mom, and they both got sent to their rooms. They just can't understand that my room is off limits for snooping.

School was so much fun today because Daisy, Lucila, and I ate lunch together outside under the trees again. We talked about the weekend, but we never mentioned the soccer game. I was expecting Lucila to brag about how she had won, but she didn't. She was acting so nice I decided not to ask Daisy if she had been trying to help Lucila win. I also got my math test back today and was so excited to see that I got a perfect score on such a hard test!

Dora

Math Test
100%

$$\frac{1}{4} + \frac{2}{4} = \frac{3}{4}$$

$$\frac{5}{7} + \frac{1}{7} = \frac{6}{7}$$

Tuesday, February 11

Dear Diary,

Right before lunch today, Mr. Fong called Lucila, Daisy, and me to his desk to tell us how proud of us he was for doing so well on our math tests. Because it was Lucila's first perfect math test score this year, Mr. Fong asked her if she had done something different to prepare for this one. Lucila's cheeks blushed as red as an apple as she told him that, actually, she and Daisy had studied for the test together over the weekend. I felt really left out because they had gotten together without telling me! I would have been very happy to study with them, so why didn't they ask me?

At lunch, Daisy and Lucila were very quiet, and I could tell they felt guilty about leaving me out. Since I always do well in math, they thought I wouldn't need to study for the test. Of course I need to study—I don't get these good scores through luck!

Dora

Wednesday, February 12

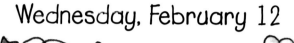

Dear Diary,

I'm having a bad afternoon. . . . No, I'm having a terrible afternoon! Lucila's mother wanted to celebrate their perfect test scores by taking Daisy and Lucila out for pizza. Lucila called to invite me to come along, but I had already promised Grandma that I would go shopping with her for a present for Omar's birthday. I would have liked to go with them, but maybe it's better that I already had other plans.

I feel kind of confused about the math test situation because I just don't understand why they would have studied without me.

Is Lucila trying to take Daisy away from me? First there was the soccer game, then studying together, and now going for pizza? It seems that they want to do everything together—and that Daisy likes Lucila more than me.

Dora

Thursday, February 13

Dear Diary,

This is turning into a really big problem, and I don't know what to do about it. I don't want to lose my two good friends—especially not Daisy—but it seems like they don't need me anymore. After thinking about it for what seemed like forever, the way I see it, I have three choices:

1. Pretend nothing has happened and act normally.
2. Stop being friends with them and find new friends.
3. Tell them how I feel and see what happens.

If I choose #1, they'll probably keep doing things without me, and I'll continue to feel left out. If I choose #2, I would really miss them, but at least I'd have other friends. If I choose #3, they might laugh at me and tell everyone. Worst of all, tomorrow is Valentine's Day, and that's a terrible day to be upset with your friends! What am I going to do?

Dora

Friday, February 14

Dear Diary,

It's Valentine's Day, but it doesn't feel like it to me. I didn't even want to go to school today, but Mom said I had to. I handed out my Valentine cards to everyone except Daisy and Lucila, and now I feel guilty. I chose not to be their friend (#2), and for a while, it felt good to pretend not to care. When they tried to talk to me at lunch, I kept playing handball with Nath and pretended I didn't hear them.

But later this afternoon, when I read the cute little card that Daisy gave me, I felt miserable. I guess Daisy left it on my seat when I went to get a drink of water. She must have known I was upset with her, yet she must have wanted me to have it anyway. The glittery, heart-shaped card said:

Dear Dora,
We are going to be best friends forever!
Happy Valentine's Day!
Daisy

Dora

Saturday, February 15

Dear Diary,

After reading this wonderful card promising that we would be friends forever, I thought that Daisy was done with show-off Lucila. I thought things would go back to normal now, but I couldn't have been more wrong! When I called Daisy tonight to ask if she wanted to go to the movies or out for pizza together, I found out the awful truth.

Daisy wanted Lucila to join us, but I said that I didn't want Lucila to come along. Daisy said that there is no reason why we all can't be good friends. She even said that I should go to the movies with them this weekend, but I was too

hurt to say yes. Can you believe what a traitor she is? We've been friends forever, and she should want to spend time with me, not with Lucila. I'm afraid that Lucila's showing off is taking Daisy away from me.

Dora

Sunday, February 16

Dear Diary,

I was so lonely this weekend without my friends, so I spent most of the time reading and following Grandpa around as he watered his garden. Mom saw that I was upset and asked what was going on with Daisy and Lucila. All I told her was that we don't talk much anymore. She said that I could have some fun with my brothers instead, so she took us to the movies. Unfortunately, it was the very same movie that Daisy and Lucila were watching!

I tried to hide by sitting far down in my chair in the back of the theater. I almost got away with it, too, until the movie ended and Omar yelled, "Hi, Daisy!" That's when things got worse because Daisy's mother and Mom started talking. I felt so uncomfortable avoiding Daisy and Lucila, and I was so embarrassed when Omar started goofing around with them. Then, unfortunately, our mothers decided to take everyone out for ice cream. . . .

Dora

Sunday, February 16, continued

Dear Diary,

I had to stop writing earlier because writing about the trip to the ice cream store was so horrible that I needed a break! My nightmare continued because the kids all sat together at one table and the adults sat at another. So there I was, between Omar and Carlos, facing the girls. Daisy and Lucila split a sundae, telling the waiter, "We want two spoons!" while I had a single scoop of vanilla in a cup, even though I had asked for a cone.

Worse yet, Omar got bubble gum ice cream and dropped four sticky pieces of blue gum on my new shirt. And Carlos's gooey banana split melted everywhere, and he piled all his sticky napkins in front of me. This had to be the most terrible, awful, embarrassing day of my life! It was bad enough that I wasn't talking to my friends, but then my brothers were messing up *everything!* I kept looking at Mom, wondering how much longer this "party" would last. My eyes felt like water balloons ready to burst, but I couldn't cry in front of everyone.

Dora

Monday, February 17

Dear Diary,

Last night, Mom said that I was not acting like myself and that I should talk to her about it. I knew she was concerned because she wanted me to tell her the whole problem, from beginning to end. She listened patiently while I told her that Lucila was trying to take Daisy away from me by showing off. I also told her that Daisy seems to like Lucila better now and only wants to spend time with her.

Mom asked what made me so sure Lucila's been trying to show off. So I told her about Lucila's soccer goals, her secret study session with Daisy, and her perfect math test score. Mom reminded me of all the good times we had together and asked if I was really willing to give all that up.

Then my mother gave me the best advice: "Dora, good friends are priceless."

Dora

Tuesday, February 18

Dear Diary,

I thought a lot about what Mom said and decided she was right: Good friends *are* hard to find. I couldn't imagine not having my friends anymore, so I decided that today I would make up with Daisy and Lucila. I was waiting until recess to talk to them, but something happened before then that changed my mind. During our reading time, I noticed that Daisy and Lucila were wearing matching friendship bracelets. Can you believe that? Friendship bracelets are the most meaningful sign of good friends that there is . . . and I don't have one!

Now I know for sure that I've lost Daisy and things will never be the same again. If it weren't for Nath sitting with me at lunch, I would have started crying. He said that I shouldn't worry and that Daisy and I would be friends again somehow. I just wondered if Daisy and Lucila would be wearing matching outfits tomorrow. Every day they seem closer to each other and farther away from me.

Dora

Wednesday, February 19

Dear Diary,

When I came home from school today, I couldn't find anything interesting to do. Finally Mom called me over to help her and Omar with a puzzle they had started. Omar was having trouble with it, but when I sat down, I started matching the pieces together quickly. Omar was amazed at how swiftly we were putting the pieces in the right places and told me I was as fast as a speeding train. I gave Omar the last piece so he would feel like he had finished it, and then the puzzle was done.

Omar said that I was really good at puzzles. Then I told him that I had a lot of practice putting them together. That's when Mom asked if I was trying to show off. Why would she think that? I wasn't trying to show off. . . . I just found all the pieces right away.

Dora

Thursday, February 20

Dear Diary,

Last night Mom and I had another long talk in my room. She asked me how I felt when she called me a show-off. I still couldn't understand why she had said that and asked her to tell me what she meant. Mom explained

that being good at something doesn't make a person a show-off.

She reminded me that I study very hard before each math test, not to show off to others, but because I want to do my best work. Mom asked me to think about Lucila's actions. Did Lucila brag about her grades and about beating me at soccer, or was she just trying to do her best? Before I write any more, I have to think about all this, so I'll let you know how I feel tomorrow.

Dora

Friday Morning, February 21

Dear Diary,

I tossed and turned most of last night, thinking about what Mom had said. Even when the lights were out and everyone else was asleep, I was still wide awake. I felt really bad about everything because I realized that it was all my fault. I guess it started because I was used to being so good at everything. I didn't like it that Lucila was better at some things than I was.

I thought more about it and realized that Lucila and Daisy *did* keep asking me to do things with them, but I was the one who said no. Lucila wasn't showing off, and Daisy wasn't choosing Lucila over me. I just made it seem that way because it felt like they didn't want my friendship anymore. After all this thinking, I finally got tired and fell asleep. Today I have to try to fix this mess.

Dora

Friday Evening, February 21

Dear Diary,

I thought it was going to be really hard to talk to Daisy and Lucila, but I'm so glad that I did! I told them that I was wrong to think that Lucila was taking Daisy away from me. Telling them I was sorry was easier than I thought it would be. Better yet, they were so glad to have me as their friend again that they didn't care about what had happened anymore!

Daisy gave me a big smile, and Lucila asked if I wanted to come study with her and Daisy at her house this weekend. We're going to study for our next math test, of course, but Lucila said that her mother might also help us do

some fun experiments with Lucila's chemistry set. I didn't know Lucila liked science, too! I can't wait to find out more about her, and I can't believe that I've wasted all this time being envious of her and Daisy.

Dora

47

Sunday, February 23

Dear Diary,

This weekend was so much fun! Daisy and Lucila made me a friendship bracelet just like theirs, and we all promised to be friends forever. I'm thrilled that Nath and Mom were right about us being friends again. And I know I'll be a much better friend from now on, for I have learned a very important lesson. I'm glad about that because otherwise, I might never have found out what great friends Lucila and Daisy are. I think we will all be friends forever!

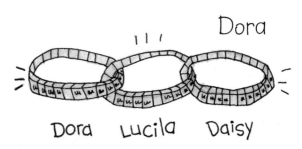

Dora

Dora Lucila Daisy